Features of the life of the Condor bird

Chapter 1: Introduction

Chapter 1: The Condor bird: A symbol of power and freedom The Condor bird is an iconic species that holds great significance in many cultures around the world. It is often regarded as a symbol of **power and freedom**, and its majestic presence is awe-inspiring to many who witness it in flight. As a psychologist, I believe that the Condor bird's symbolism reflects our innate **desire for strength and independence**. Its soaring flight represents the ability to rise above adversity and see things from a higher perspective. In some cultures, the Condor bird is also associated with **spiritual or supernatural powers**, such as the ability to communicate with the divine or access hidden knowledge. This highlights the deep respect and reverence that many people hold for this magnificent creature. However, despite its symbolic importance, the Condor bird faces many challenges in the modern world, including habitat loss, hunting, and poisoning from lead ammunition. It is up to us to protect and preserve this remarkable species for future generations to appreciate and admire.

Chapter 2: Purpose and scope of the book This book, "Features of the life of the Condor bird," aims to provide a **comprehensive overview** of this magnificent species and its unique characteristics. Through this book, we hope to educate readers about the Condor bird's **behavior, ecology, and cultural significance**, as well as the challenges it faces in the modern world. As a ornithologist, I believe that learning about the Condor bird can have many benefits for human well-being. Studies have shown that exposure to nature and wildlife can **reduce stress, increase feelings of happiness and connectedness**, and promote environmental awareness and conservation efforts. Moreover, understanding the Condor bird's **ecology and conservation challenges** can inspire us to take action to protect this species and its habitat. By learning about the Condor bird's **cultural significance**, we can gain a deeper appreciation for the ways in which nature and human culture are interconnected. Overall, the purpose of this book is to celebrate the Condor bird's unique features and inspire readers to take an active role in protecting this magnificent species. We hope that readers will come away from this book with a renewed sense of wonder and respect for the natural world.

Chapter 3: Overview of the Condor bird's habitat and distribution The Condor bird is native to the Americas and is found primarily in **mountainous regions**. Its habitat ranges from the Andes mountains in South America to the coastal mountains of California in North America. As a ornithologist, I believe that understanding the Condor bird's habitat and distribution is crucial for its conservation. The Condor bird requires large, open spaces to forage and roost, and it is particularly dependent on the presence of large trees for nesting. Historically, the Condor bird's range extended from Canada to South America, but today, its population is much smaller and fragmented. The Condor bird has been extirpated from many areas due to habitat loss, hunting, and poisoning from lead ammunition. Conservation efforts have been successful in some areas, and the Condor bird's population has begun to recover. However, continued conservation efforts are needed to protect the Condor bird and its habitat.

By learning about the Condor bird's habitat and distribution, we can work to ensure that this magnificent species continues to thrive for generations to come.

Chapter 2: Physical Characteristics

Anatomy and morphology of the Condor bird

The Condor bird is a large bird of prey that is known for its impressive size and striking appearance. As an ornithologist, I find the anatomy and morphology of the Condor bird to be fascinating and unique. The Condor bird has a wingspan of up to 10 feet, which makes it one of the largest flying birds in the world. Its body is covered in black feathers, and it has a distinctive white ruff of feathers around its neck. The head and neck are featherless and colored in shades of pink, red, and orange. The beak of the Condor bird is hooked and strong, which allows it to tear through tough meat and carrion. Its talons are also powerful and are used to grip and carry prey. The Condor bird's eyesight is exceptional and is used to spot prey from great distances. The anatomy and morphology of the Condor bird have evolved to make it a highly efficient predator and scavenger. Its large size and powerful beak and talons allow it to hunt and consume a wide variety of prey, while its exceptional eyesight enables it to spot carrion from great distances. Understanding the anatomy and morphology of the Condor bird is essential for appreciating its unique characteristics and the role it plays in its ecosystem. By studying the physical traits of the Condor bird, we can gain insight into how it has adapted to its environment and how it continues to thrive despite the challenges it faces.

Unique adaptations for flight and survival

As an ornithologist, I am constantly amazed by the unique adaptations that birds have developed to survive in their environments. The Condor bird, in particular, has evolved several fascinating adaptations that have enabled it to thrive in the harsh conditions of its habitat. One of the most remarkable adaptations of the Condor bird is its ability to soar for long periods without flapping its wings. It achieves this by taking advantage of rising air currents called thermals. The Condor bird will fly in circles within these thermals, allowing it to gain altitude and travel long distances with minimal effort. Another unique adaptation of the Condor bird is its ability to consume carrion that has started to decay. This is made possible by its strong digestive system, which can break down bacteria and toxins that would be deadly to other animals. The Condor bird also has a keen sense of smell, which allows it to locate carrion from great distances. The Condor bird's feathers are also uniquely adapted for flight and survival. They are incredibly strong and flexible, which allows the bird to maintain its balance and control during flight. Additionally, the feathers are arranged in such a way that they create a smooth surface that reduces air resistance, allowing the bird to fly more efficiently. In summary, the Condor bird has evolved several unique adaptations that enable it to survive and thrive in its harsh environment. Its ability to soar for long periods without flapping its wings, consume decaying carrion, and its strong feathers are all critical adaptations for its survival. As an ornithologist, I am constantly in awe of the incredible adaptations that birds have developed to succeed in their environments.

Sexual dimorphism and breeding biology

Condors exhibit sexual dimorphism, with males typically being larger than females. The males can weigh up to 33 pounds and have a wingspan of up to 10 feet, while females can weigh up to 24 pounds and have a wingspan of up to 9 feet.

The breeding biology of condors is fascinating. These birds typically mate for life, and both parents share in the responsibilities of raising their young. Females usually lay a single egg every two years, and both parents take turns incubating the egg for about two months. Once the egg hatches, both parents feed and care for the chick, which will remain in the nest for up to six months.

While condors may not breed as frequently as some other bird species, their dedication to their offspring is remarkable. It is not uncommon for parents to continue caring for their young even after they have left the nest, and juveniles may stay with their parents for several years before establishing their own territories.

As an ornithologist, I find the breeding biology of condors to be truly remarkable. Their commitment to their young and long-term pair bonds demonstrate the complexity and depth of their social behavior, which is often overlooked when considering these birds solely for their physical characteristics.

Chapter 3: Behavior and Social Structure

Feeding Habits and Dietary Preferences

Condors are carrion feeders, which means that they feed on the carcasses of dead animals. They have a highly developed sense of smell that helps them locate dead animals from great distances. Condors have also been observed to scavenge on garbage dumps, which can be harmful to their health due to the ingestion of plastic and other non-biodegradable materials.

Condors are opportunistic feeders and will eat a variety of carcasses, including those of mammals, birds, and reptiles. They are known to prefer larger animals, such as deer and cattle, but will also feed on smaller animals such as rodents and rabbits. Condors are also known to steal food from other scavengers such as vultures and eagles, and have been observed to follow predators such as coyotes and foxes in order to scavenge on their kills.

As a ornithologist, I find it fascinating how the feeding habits of condors have evolved to allow them to survive in their natural habitat. Their ability to locate and consume carrion plays a vital role in maintaining the ecological balance of their environment, as it helps to prevent the spread of disease from decaying animal carcasses.

Courtship and Mating Rituals

The courtship and mating rituals of the Condor bird are fascinating to observe. The process starts with the male performing an elaborate dance to attract a female. The male spreads his wings and jumps into the air, displaying his impressive size and wingspan.

Once a female has been attracted, the pair engage in a courtship ritual that involves various behaviors, such as circling each other in the air, soaring together, and sharing food. The bonding process is essential for the success of the pair, as Condors mate for life.

The breeding season of the Condor bird varies depending on their location, but it typically occurs between September and March. The female lays one egg, and both parents take turns incubating it. The egg hatches after around 56 days, and the chick is born blind and helpless. It relies entirely on its parents for food and care, and the pair work together to ensure the chick's survival.

The courtship and mating rituals of the Condor bird are not only essential for reproduction but also serve to strengthen the bonds between the pair. It is fascinating to witness the elaborate displays of affection between these magnificent birds, which have evolved over time to ensure the survival of their species.

Nesting Behavior and Parental Care

Nesting behavior and parental care are crucial aspects of the life of the Condor bird.

Nesting Behavior

The Condor bird builds its nests on rocky ledges, cliffs, or in caves. The nest is made of sticks and other vegetation, and can measure up to 10 feet in width and 5 feet in height. The female lays one or two eggs, which are incubated by both parents for approximately 55-60 days.

Once the chicks hatch, they are completely dependent on their parents for food and protection. The parents regurgitate food for the chicks, and also protect them from predators such as eagles and foxes.

Parental Care

Condor parents are highly dedicated to their offspring and provide extensive parental care. Both parents take turns incubating the eggs and protecting the chicks. They also feed the chicks by regurgitating food, and will continue to do so for several months after the chicks have fledged.

Parental care is especially important for the survival of the Condor bird, which has a low reproductive rate and slow growth rate. The parents must invest a lot of time and energy into their offspring to ensure their survival.

In addition to parental care, conservation efforts have also played a role in protecting and preserving the Condor bird population.

In conclusion, nesting behavior and parental care are crucial for the survival of the Condor bird. These birds exhibit remarkable dedication and care for their offspring, which is essential for the continuation of the species.

Interactions with other Condor birds and species

Condor birds are social animals that interact with other members of their species in various ways. One of the most important interactions is during breeding season when they form pairs for mating and raising their young. However, they also engage in social interactions such as preening, allopreening, and vocalizations.

Condor birds are also part of the larger ecosystem and interact with other species in their habitat. They are apex predators and play a crucial role in controlling populations of smaller animals. However, they can also be affected by other species, particularly those that prey on their young or compete with them for food resources.

Human activities also have a significant impact on condor birds and their interactions with other species. Habitat destruction, hunting, and poaching can all disrupt the delicate balance of the ecosystem and affect the survival of condor birds and other species in their habitat. Conservation efforts are crucial to protecting these majestic birds and their interactions with other species in the wild.

Chapter 4: Ecology and Conservation

Habitat Requirements and Distribution Patterns

The Andean condor is found primarily in South America, ranging from Venezuela in the north to Tierra del Fuego in the south. They are most commonly found in the Andes Mountains, where they make their nests in cliffs and other high elevations.

The Andean condor requires a specific type of habitat to survive. They are most commonly found in areas with high elevations, low humidity, and strong winds. These conditions provide the ideal environment for soaring and gliding, which the condor uses to travel long distances in search of food.

The condor's diet consists mainly of carrion, or the carcasses of dead animals. As a result, they are often found near areas with large populations of wild herbivores, such as llamas and guanacos. They are also known to scavenge near human settlements and landfills.

While the Andean condor is not considered to be endangered, their population has declined in recent years due to habitat loss, hunting, and poisoning. Conservation efforts are underway to protect the species and ensure their continued survival.

As an ornithologist, it is important to study the habitat requirements and distribution patterns of the Andean condor in order to better understand their behavior and develop effective conservation strategies. By working to protect their habitat and reduce human impact on their environment, we can help ensure that this magnificent bird continues to thrive for generations to come.

Threats to the Condor Bird's Survival

As an ornithologist, it is important to understand the threats to the survival of the Condor bird. These threats include:

Hunting and poaching

The Condor bird was once heavily hunted for its feathers, which were used in Native American rituals and ceremonies. This hunting, combined with habitat destruction, led to a significant decline in the Condor bird population. Although hunting is now illegal, there have been instances of poaching, and some individuals still view the Condor bird as a target for sport.

Habitat loss and fragmentation

Condor birds require large areas of open space to hunt and breed. However, habitat loss due to human activities such as agriculture, mining, and urbanization has reduced the amount of suitable habitat available for these birds. Habitat fragmentation, which occurs when large areas of habitat are broken up into smaller patches, also poses a significant threat to the Condor bird's survival.

Lead poisoning

Condor birds are scavengers, and they often consume the remains of animals that have been shot with lead bullets. This can lead to lead poisoning, which can be fatal to the birds. Efforts have been made to reduce the use of lead ammunition in areas where Condor birds are known to live, but the risk of lead poisoning remains a significant threat.

Electric power lines and wind turbines

Condor birds are at risk of colliding with power lines and wind turbines, which can cause injury or death. Efforts have been made to reduce the risk of collision, such as marking power lines with visible markers and placing wind turbines away from Condor bird habitats, but these efforts are not always successful.

Climate change

Climate change poses a threat to the Condor bird's survival by altering the birds' habitats and food sources. As temperatures rise and precipitation patterns change, the availability of suitable habitat and prey may be reduced, which could have a negative impact on the Condor bird population.

It is important for conservationists and policymakers to work together to address these threats and protect the Condor bird's habitat and population. By taking action to reduce hunting, preserve habitat, and reduce the risk of lead poisoning and collisions, we can help ensure that these magnificent birds continue to thrive for generations to come.

Conservation efforts and success stories

As an ornithologist, I am keenly aware of the threats facing the Condor bird and the need for conservation efforts to protect this magnificent species. Fortunately, there have been some successful conservation efforts that have helped to increase the population of the Condor bird. One of the biggest threats to the Condor bird is habitat loss. With the destruction of forests and other natural habitats, the Condor bird is losing its home and food sources. Conservation organizations have been working hard to protect the Condor bird's habitat by preserving forests and other natural areas. In addition, captive breeding programs have been established to help increase the population of the Condor bird. Another major threat to the Condor bird is hunting. In the past, the Condor bird was hunted for its feathers, which were used for decorative purposes. Today, hunting is illegal, but some people still poach the

Condor bird for its meat or body parts, which are believed to have medicinal properties. Conservation organizations are working with law enforcement agencies to crack down on poaching and protect the Condor bird from this threat. Conservation efforts have been successful in increasing the population of the Condor bird in some areas. For example, in California, the population of the Condor bird has increased from only 27 birds in the 1980s to over 400 birds today. This success is due in part to the captive breeding program that was established in the 1980s to help increase the population of the Condor bird. Another success story is in the Andes Mountains, where the population of the Condor bird has been increasing thanks to conservation efforts. In Peru, the government has established protected areas for the Condor bird, and conservation organizations have been working to educate local communities about the importance of protecting this species. In conclusion, the Condor bird is facing significant threats to its survival, but there is hope.

Through conservation efforts such as protecting habitats, captive breeding programs, and cracking down on poaching, the population of the Condor bird has been increasing in some areas. With continued effort and dedication, we can ensure that this magnificent species continues to thrive for generations to come.

Chapter 5: Historical and Cultural Significance

Role of the Condor bird in indigenous and modern cultures

As an ornithologist, I find it fascinating how the Condor bird has played an important role in the cultures of the Andean people for centuries. The indigenous people of the Andes saw the Condor as a sacred bird that represented the spirit of the mountains and the sky. The bird was often depicted in their art and mythology as a powerful and wise creature.

The Condor has also played a role in modern cultures, particularly in the countries where it is found, such as Peru, Bolivia, Chile, and Argentina. In these countries, the Condor is a national symbol and is featured on their flags and coat of arms.

But the Condor's cultural significance extends beyond just being a symbol. The bird has been a source of inspiration for many artists, musicians, and writers. Its majestic presence and unique adaptations for flight have captured the imagination of people all over the world.

However, the Condor's cultural significance also brings attention to the need for conservation efforts to protect this iconic species. The decline of the Condor population due to habitat loss and hunting has not only threatened the species but also the cultural significance it holds.

Conservation efforts have been put in place to protect the Condor and its habitat. The reintroduction of captive-bred Condors into the wild has been a success story in some areas. These efforts have not only helped to increase the population of the species but also to preserve its cultural significance for generations to come.

In conclusion, the Condor bird's cultural significance is a testament to its remarkable adaptations and unique presence in the Andean ecosystems. Its importance in indigenous and modern cultures highlights the need for conservation efforts to ensure the survival of this iconic species and its cultural significance.

Historical Accounts and Myths Surrounding the Condor Bird

Throughout history, the Condor bird has held a special place in the culture and mythology of the people who live in its range. From ancient times to modern day, the bird has been revered as a symbol of power, freedom, and spirituality. In this chapter, we will explore some of the historical accounts and myths surrounding the Condor bird.

Ancient Times

The Condor bird has been a part of the cultural history of the Andean people for thousands of years. The Inca civilization, which ruled over much of South America in the 15th and 16th centuries, considered the Condor to be a sacred bird. According to Inca mythology, the Condor was one of the messengers of the sun god Inti, and its ability to soar high into the sky was seen as a symbol of spiritual transcendence.

The Moche people, who lived in what is now modern-day Peru from around 100 BCE to 800 CE, also had a close relationship with the Condor. They depicted the bird in their art and pottery, and it was believed to be a symbol of power and strength. In Moche mythology, the Condor was a powerful creature that could fly between the world of the living and the dead.

Modern Times

Today, the Condor bird remains an important symbol in the culture and mythology of the Andean people. It is often depicted in artwork, textiles, and other crafts, and its image can be found on flags and other national symbols.

But the bird has also taken on a new meaning in modern times. As one of the largest and most majestic birds in the world, the Condor has become a symbol of conservation and the fight to protect endangered species. In many countries, efforts are being made to preserve the bird's habitat and increase its population.

Conclusion

Throughout history, the Condor bird has held a special place in the culture and mythology of the Andean people. Its ability to soar high into the sky has been seen as a symbol of power, freedom, and spirituality. Today, the bird remains an important symbol in the fight to protect endangered species and preserve the environment for future generations.

Symbolic Meanings and Interpretations

Throughout history, the Condor bird has held a significant place in the cultures and spiritual beliefs of the people who share its habitat. From ancient times to the present day, the Condor has been revered as a symbol of power, freedom, and wisdom.

Indigenous cultures

Indigenous cultures in South America have long regarded the Condor as a sacred bird. For the Inca people, the Condor represented the heavens and was believed to possess the power of flight over both the physical and spiritual realms. They believed that the Condor was a messenger of the gods and could communicate with them through its high-flying flights.

The Mapuche people of Chile and Argentina also view the Condor as a symbol of spiritual power. They believe that the Condor has the power to carry their prayers and messages to the heavens and to bring back blessings from the gods.

Modern cultures

The Condor bird's symbolic meaning has not been limited to indigenous cultures, but also extended to modern cultures. In modern times, the Condor bird has come to symbolize freedom, strength, and resilience. For example, the emblem of the nation of Colombia features a Condor bird in flight, representing the nation's freedom and power.

The Condor bird has also become a symbol of conservation and environmental protection. Due to their importance as a top predator in the ecosystem and their cultural significance, efforts have been made to protect their habitats and conserve their populations. By doing so, we are preserving not only the bird species but also the symbolic meanings associated with them.

Mythical interpretations

Throughout history, the Condor has also been the subject of many myths and legends. In some myths, the Condor was believed to be a powerful shapeshifter, capable of changing its form to become a human or an animal. In other myths, the Condor was seen as a symbol of death and rebirth, as it was believed to consume the flesh of the dead and then release their spirits into the heavens.

While these myths may not be based on scientific fact, they do serve to highlight the deep cultural significance of the Condor bird in the human imagination.

Conclusion

The Condor bird has played a significant role in the cultures and spiritual beliefs of people throughout history. Its symbolic meanings have evolved and expanded, but its power and importance have remained constant. By protecting the habitats and populations of these magnificent birds, we are not only preserving a species, but also a symbol of freedom, strength, and wisdom that has endured for thousands of years.

Chapter 6: Research and Field Studies

Techniques and Methods for Studying the Condor Bird in the Wild

Studying the Condor bird in the wild is a challenging task due to its remote and often inaccessible habitats. However, with the advancement of technology and scientific techniques, researchers have developed various methods to study these birds.

Field Observations

Field observations are one of the most common methods used by ornithologists to study the Condor bird. This method involves observing the bird's behavior and recording it in a notebook or on a digital device. Observations can be made from a distance using binoculars or spotting scopes, or by getting closer to the bird using blinds or hides.

Field observations can provide valuable information on the bird's behavior, such as feeding, courtship, and nesting habits. However, this method has its limitations as it may not capture all aspects of the bird's behavior and may be influenced by the observer's bias.

Radio Telemetry

Radio telemetry is another method used to study the Condor bird. This technique involves attaching a small transmitter to the bird's body and tracking its movements using a receiver. This method is particularly useful for studying the bird's movements and habitat use.

Radio telemetry has enabled researchers to understand the bird's foraging behavior, migration patterns, and habitat preferences. However, this method is expensive and requires a team of trained researchers to track and monitor the bird's movements.

Genetic Analysis

Genetic analysis is a powerful tool used to study the genetic diversity, relatedness, and population structure of the Condor bird. This method involves collecting tissue or blood samples from the bird and analyzing the DNA to extract genetic information.

Genetic analysis has provided valuable insights into the bird's population genetics, including the level of genetic diversity, the existence of subpopulations, and the level of inbreeding. This method has also helped researchers to identify parentage and relatedness among individuals.

Remote Sensing

Remote sensing is a method used to study the Condor bird's habitat use and distribution. This method involves using satellite imagery or aerial photography to map the bird's habitat and analyze landscape features.

Remote sensing has provided valuable information on the bird's habitat preferences and distribution, including the identification of critical habitat areas and the impact of landscape changes on the bird's habitat.

Conclusion

Studying the Condor bird in the wild is a complex task that requires a combination of scientific techniques and methods. Field observations, radio telemetry, genetic analysis, and remote sensing are some of the most common methods used to study these birds. These methods have provided valuable insights into the bird's behavior, ecology, and conservation, and have helped to inform management decisions aimed at protecting this iconic species.

Current Research Questions and Findings

As a ornithologist, I am always interested in the latest research on the Condor bird. There are many ongoing studies that aim to expand our knowledge about this magnificent species. One important area of research focuses on the genetic diversity of the Condor bird population. Scientists are studying the genetic makeup of Condor populations in different regions to determine the level of genetic diversity within the species. This research is important because genetic diversity is crucial for the long-term survival of a species. Another important research question is how the Condor bird uses thermals for flight. Thermals are columns of rising air that birds can use to gain altitude without expending much energy. Scientists are using high-tech instruments like GPS and accelerometers to track the flight patterns of Condor birds and study how they use thermals to stay aloft for long periods of time.

Researchers are also studying the microbiome of the Condor bird. The microbiome refers to the microorganisms that live within an animal's body. This research is important because the microbiome plays a crucial role in an animal's overall health and wellbeing. One fascinating recent finding is that Condor birds use social cues to find food. Scientists have discovered that when one Condor finds food, it emits a specific call that alerts other Condors in the area. This behavior, known as "scavenging for information," allows the birds to work together to locate food sources more efficiently. There is also ongoing research on the effects of lead poisoning on Condor birds. Lead poisoning is a major threat to Condor bird populations, and scientists are studying how to minimize the risks of lead exposure. Overall, these research questions and findings demonstrate the ongoing efforts to better understand and protect the Condor bird. By staying up-to-date on the latest research, we can continue to develop effective conservation strategies to ensure the long-term survival of this magnificent species.

Future Directions for Research and Conservation Efforts

As an ornithologist, I believe that there is still much to learn about the Condor bird, and that future research will be crucial to its survival. One area of research that should be explored is the impact of climate change on the bird's habitat and food sources. With temperatures rising, and weather patterns changing, it is likely that the Condor's environment will be affected, and this could have serious consequences for its survival. Another area of research that should be explored is the bird's behavior and breeding habits. Understanding these patterns can help conservationists develop better management strategies for protecting the species. For example, knowing when and where the birds prefer to nest can help land managers create protected areas and implement conservation practices in these locations. In terms of conservation efforts, it is essential that we continue to work to protect the Condor bird and its habitat. This includes efforts to reduce habitat loss, combat poaching and hunting, and manage captive breeding programs. Collaboration between government agencies, non-profit organizations, and private individuals will be crucial to these efforts. One promising development in recent years has been the use of satellite technology to track the movements of Condor birds. This has allowed researchers to better understand the bird's range and behavior, and can inform conservation efforts. Additionally, advances in DNA analysis and other technologies may provide new insights into the bird's genetic makeup, which could inform conservation strategies. Ultimately, the survival of the Condor bird will depend on our ability to work together to protect it and its habitat. Through continued research and conservation efforts, we can ensure that this magnificent bird will continue to soar over our skies for generations to come.

Chapter 7: Captive Breeding and Rehabilitation

Challenges and successes of captive breeding programs

As an ornithologist, I have seen first-hand the challenges and successes of captive breeding programs for the conservation of endangered bird species such as the condor. Captive breeding programs are one of the many methods used in conservation efforts to help recover populations of endangered species. One of the biggest challenges faced by captive breeding programs is genetic diversity. In small captive populations, the gene pool can become limited, leading to inbreeding depression and reduced genetic fitness. To counteract this, breeding programs aim to create genetic diversity through careful pairing and genetic management. Another challenge is ensuring the animals remain healthy and have a natural environment in captivity. Captive breeding facilities must provide adequate space, diet, and medical care to ensure the birds thrive. Additionally, the birds must be able to exhibit natural behaviors such as foraging, preening, and socializing. Despite these challenges, captive breeding programs have had many successes in the conservation of endangered species. The California Condor, for example, was once down to only 27 individuals in the wild. Through captive breeding efforts, the population has increased to over 400 individuals, with over 200 living in the wild. Another success story is the Mauritius Kestrel, a bird once thought to be extinct. Captive breeding efforts helped to re-establish a population in the wild, with the current population estimated to be around 800 individuals. Captive breeding programs can also aid in the reintroduction of species to their natural habitats. Once the population has reached a certain size and genetic diversity has been established, birds can be released back into the wild. This process, known as reintroduction, can be a critical step in conserving endangered species. In conclusion, captive breeding programs play an important role in conservation efforts for endangered bird species such as the condor. While there are certainly challenges, successes such as the California Condor and Mauritius Kestrel demonstrate the positive impact that captive breeding programs can have on the conservation of endangered species.

Techniques for rehabilitating injured or orphaned Condor birds

As an ornithologist, one of the most important aspects of my work is helping injured or orphaned Condor birds return to the wild. Rehabilitation is a delicate process that requires a combination of scientific knowledge, technical skills, and a deep understanding of the needs of these majestic birds. One of the first steps in rehabilitating an injured Condor bird is to determine the extent of their injuries. This involves a thorough physical examination and diagnostic testing such as radiographs and blood work. Once the bird's injuries have been assessed, a treatment plan can be developed to address their specific needs. In some cases, injured Condor birds may need surgery to repair broken bones or other injuries. This requires a skilled veterinary team with experience working with birds of prey. After surgery, the bird is placed in a specially designed enclosure where they can rest and recover. Orphaned Condor chicks require a different approach to rehabilitation. These birds are typically raised in captivity until they are old enough to be released into the wild. During this time, they are taught critical skills such as flying, foraging for food, and socializing with other Condors. This process is known as "hacking," and it is essential to ensure the bird's survival once they are released into the wild. Another important aspect of rehabilitating Condor birds is providing them with a proper diet. In captivity, these birds are fed a diet that closely resembles their natural diet in the wild. This typically includes a variety of meats, such as beef, rabbit, and quail. In addition, birds are supplemented with vitamins and minerals to ensure they are receiving all of the necessary nutrients for optimal health. Successful rehabilitation of Condor birds requires a combination of technical expertise, scientific knowledge, and a deep commitment to the welfare of these magnificent birds. With the right care and attention, injured or orphaned Condor birds can make a full recovery and return to the wild where they belong.

Release and Monitoring of Rehabilitated Birds in the Wild

As an ornithologist, one of the most rewarding aspects of my job is being involved in the release and monitoring of rehabilitated Condor birds. After an injured or orphaned bird has received medical treatment and been deemed healthy enough for release, the next step is to carefully prepare the bird for life in the wild. The release process involves more than simply opening a cage and letting the bird go. Careful planning and preparation are necessary to give the bird the best chance of survival. Birds are typically released in areas where they are known to have lived in the past, or in areas where they are likely to find a mate and establish a new territory. Monitoring the released birds is crucial to ensuring their success. Tracking devices are often used to monitor the movements and behavior of released birds. This information can help researchers better understand how the birds are adapting to their new environment and identify any challenges they may be facing. One of the biggest challenges facing rehabilitated Condor birds is the potential lack of socialization with other birds. In some cases, birds that have spent a significant amount of time in captivity may struggle to establish social relationships with other birds in the wild. This can make it difficult for them to find a mate and reproduce, which is essential for the long-term success of the species. To address this challenge, some rehabilitation programs use a "soft release" technique, which involves gradually acclimating the bird to its new environment over a period of time. This allows the bird to establish social relationships with other birds and become more familiar with its surroundings before being fully released into the wild. The success of rehabilitation and release programs for Condor birds is a testament to the dedication and hard work of the many people involved. From veterinarians and biologists to volunteers and donors, it takes a coordinated effort to ensure the survival of this magnificent species. In conclusion, the release and monitoring of rehabilitated Condor birds is a critical component of conservation efforts for this species. By carefully preparing birds for release and monitoring their success in the wild, researchers can gain valuable insights into the behavior and needs of these remarkable birds. With continued dedication and collaboration, we can ensure a bright future for the Condor bird.

Chapter 8: Conclusion

Summary of key points and insights

As an ornithologist, I have shared many facts, insights, and opinions about the Condor bird in this book. Here are some of the key points that we have covered:

- The Condor bird is one of the largest flying birds in the world and is a fascinating species to study and observe.

- Condors are found in the western coastal mountains of North and South America, and they have a range of interesting adaptations and behaviors that help them survive in these environments.

- The Condor bird has played an important role in the mythologies and cultures of the indigenous peoples of the Andes and other regions where it is found.

- Despite its cultural significance, the Condor bird faces many challenges, including habitat loss, hunting, and poisoning from lead ammunition.

- Captive breeding programs have been successful in helping to increase the numbers of Condor birds in the wild, but these programs face many challenges, including genetic issues and difficulty in finding suitable release sites.

- Rehabilitation of injured or orphaned Condor birds is an important part of conservation efforts, and techniques such as wing repair surgery and chick rearing by foster parents have been developed to aid in this effort.

- Monitoring of released birds is essential to track their survival and reproduction, and techniques such as radio telemetry and GPS tracking have been developed to aid in this effort.

- There are many research questions still to be answered about the behavior, ecology, and genetics of the Condor bird, and continued research efforts are important for the conservation of this species.

Overall, the Condor bird is a fascinating and important species, and there is much work to be done to ensure its survival and well-being in the wild. By learning more about this species and working to protect it, we can help to ensure that it continues to be a part of our natural world for generations to come.

Reflections on the Importance of Studying and Protecting the Condor Bird

As an ornithologist who has dedicated my life to studying and protecting birds, the Condor bird holds a special place in my heart. The majestic bird is not only a symbol of strength and freedom, but also an important part of our ecosystem. In this final chapter, I want to reflect on the importance of studying and protecting the Condor bird, and why we must continue to work towards their conservation.

The Ecological Importance of the Condor Bird

Condors play a critical role in maintaining the balance of our ecosystem. As scavengers, they help to keep our environment clean by feeding on carrion, which helps to prevent the spread of diseases. Their presence in the wild also supports other wildlife by providing a food source for predators such as coyotes and bears. Therefore, the extinction of the Condor bird would have a ripple effect on the entire ecosystem, disrupting the balance that has existed for centuries.

The Cultural Significance of the Condor Bird

The Condor bird holds a significant place in the cultural and spiritual beliefs of indigenous communities throughout its range. Many indigenous cultures see the Condor bird as a sacred animal, representing strength, wisdom, and freedom. The extinction of the Condor bird would not only impact the ecosystem, but also the cultural heritage of these communities.

The Threats Facing the Condor Bird

The Condor bird faces a number of threats, including habitat loss, hunting, and poisoning from lead ammunition. In addition, climate change and environmental pollution also pose significant risks to the survival of this species. Without intervention, the population of the Condor bird could continue to decline, leading to the eventual extinction of the species.

The Importance of Conservation Efforts

Conservation efforts have played a critical role in the recovery of the Condor bird population. Captive breeding programs have helped to increase the number of Condor birds in the wild, while rehabilitation and release programs have helped to care for injured or orphaned birds. However, continued efforts are needed to address the ongoing threats facing the species and to ensure its survival.

Final Thoughts

The Condor bird is not only a symbol of freedom and strength, but also an important part of our ecosystem and cultural heritage. As ornithologists, it is our responsibility to continue studying and protecting this species, and to ensure that future generations can appreciate its majesty and significance. By working together, we can help to secure a brighter future for the Condor bird and all the wildlife that depends on it.

Call to action for conservation and education efforts

As an ornithologist, I have seen firsthand the importance of conservation efforts for the Condor bird. The Condor is a keystone species in its ecosystem, meaning that its presence is crucial for maintaining the balance of the ecosystem. Without the Condor, other species may become overpopulated or even go extinct, leading to a chain reaction of negative consequences.

It is important for individuals and organizations to take action to protect the Condor bird and its habitat. This can include supporting conservation organizations that work to protect the bird and its environment, advocating for legislation that protects the bird and its habitat, and educating others about the importance of conservation efforts.

Education is particularly important in conservation efforts, as it helps people understand the value of protecting the Condor bird and its ecosystem. By raising awareness about the bird and its role in the ecosystem, we can inspire people to take action to protect it.

It is also important to support efforts to rehabilitate and release injured or orphaned Condor birds back into the wild. Rehabilitation and release programs can help increase the population of the bird in the wild, and give injured or orphaned birds a second chance at life.

Ultimately, the survival of the Condor bird depends on the actions we take today. We have the power to protect and conserve this incredible species, and by doing so, we can ensure a healthy and balanced ecosystem for generations to come.

So I urge you, as readers of this book, to take action and support conservation efforts for the Condor bird. Together, we can make a difference and help protect this magnificent bird and its ecosystem.